Mission Given, Mission Accomplished

Special Forces Strategies for Building High-Performance Teams in Corporate Management.

Paulo Ehms

MMXXIII

Table of Contents

Introduction

Mission Given, Mission Accomplished: Special Forces Strategies for Building High-Performance Teams in Corporate Management.

In a world where competitiveness is the norm and success is defined by adaptability, there is an incessant search for methods that elevate teams to excellence. This book proposes a unique approach, where elite strategies of special forces meet corporate corridors, forming an unparalleled alliance of leadership and effectiveness.

Imagine a mission where excellence is the only option, where each team member is a vital piece in a complex puzzle. In special forces, the mission given is the mission accomplished, and each operation is a choreographed dance of skill, resilience, and precise communication.

Now, transpose this scenario into the business world. Here, teams are operational units, managers are commanders, and each challenge is a mission to be accomplished. In "Mission Given, Mission Accomplished," we will explore how the principles of special forces become essential tools for forging teams that not only meet but exceed expectations.

Throughout these pages, we will delve into the essence of effective leadership, communication that transcends barriers, and resilience that transforms challenges into opportunities. Each chapter is a mission, each lesson an achievement, and the mission is clear: to form high-performance teams that will be the best of the best.

Are you ready to embark on this journey where the battlefield is the office, and victory is measured by lasting success? Let's begin this mission together.

Chapter 1

Legendary Roots: From Mythical Troops to Contemporary Heroes

In the deepest corners of history, where myths dance with reality, we find the legendary roots that gave rise to modern special forces. This chapter invites us on a journey through the centuries, exploring the legends of the Ancient Greek Myrmidons and the Roman Empire's Praetorians, where courage blends with discipline, and indomitable fury meets unwavering loyalty.

First Steps: Emergence and Necessity of Special Forces

Before being recorded in scrolls and manuscripts, the seeds of special forces were sown on primeval battlefields. In the early conflicts, unique challenges arose that demanded innovative responses. Need, the mother of invention, gave birth to the creation of the first specialized units.

The Early Days of War: Unique Challenges Demand Special Responses

In the chaotic setting of early wars, with unpredictable terrains and unconventional tactics, the demand for a more efficient response grew. Battles were not just between armies but between adaptability and rigidity. In this context, the first special forces emerged to confront enemies and challenges that eluded traditional strategies.

Innovation and Adaptability: The First Seeds of Special Forces

The response to the emerging need was military innovation. The first special units were composed of skilled and adaptable warriors, chosen not only for their brute strength but for their ability to think beyond conventional lines. Their tactics were shaped by flexibility, allowing quick and effective responses to challenging scenarios.

The Call of the Myrmidons: Discipline in the Trojan War

As the dust of the early war settled, a group of warriors emerged who embodied discipline and unwavering determination: the Myrmidons. Led by Achilles, whose name was synonymous with invincibility, the Myrmidons were a unique force in the Trojan War.

Achilles and Unyielding Discipline

Achilles, the fearless leader of the Myrmidons, stood out not only for his combat skills but for the discipline he instilled in his troop. Each Myrmidon was trained to follow orders with military precision, without hesitation. The discipline of the Myrmidons was not just a formality; it was the backbone that supported the effectiveness and cohesion of the unit.

Discipline Beyond Mortality

The discipline of the Myrmidons transcended the bounds of mortality. Amidst the chaos of war, Achilles demanded perfection from his warriors, creating a cohesive and resilient unit that faced challenges that seemed insurmountable. The Myrmidons embodied not only physical strength but also the ability to maintain composure and efficiency under the most extreme conditions. By traversing the battlefields of the Trojan War, we explore the call of the Myrmidons, revealing how discipline became the foundation of a legend that would echo through the centuries. Let us embark together on this journey, where war becomes a stage for the forging of exceptional warriors.

The Roman Vanguard

Praetorians as Guardians of the Emperor

While the Myrmidons left their mark in the sands of Antiquity, in the depths of the Roman Empire emerged a force whose unwavering loyalty would become legendary: the Praetorians. Designated as the elite guard of the emperor, they not only faced external threats but also played a vital role in maintaining the stability and internal security of the empire.

Stringent Selection and Exhaustive Training

The Praetorians were not simple soldiers; they were chosen from the best of the Roman legions. Under a rigorous selection process, only the most skilled and loyal were admitted. Their training knew no bounds, encompassing advanced military strategies, close combat techniques, and personal defense tactics. They became masters of the art of war and personal protection.

Unyielding Guardians of Imperial Power

The fundamental mission of the Praetorians was clear: to ensure the direct security of the emperor and his family. In addition to their imposing presence in ceremonies and official events, they were the last line of defense against internal threats. Their loyalty, often sworn in solemn oaths, was an unbreakable commitment to the person of the emperor and the stability of the empire.

The Emperor as the Central Focus

Unlike regular legions, the Praetorians were not just a military force. They were an institution that personified the direct connection between the emperor and his power. The trust placed in them was evident, and their constant presence was a visual reminder of the inseparable bond between the supreme leader and his personal guard.

Enduring Impact on Military History

The legacy of the Praetorians transcended the borders of the Roman Empire. Their organizational structure and the idea of an elite guard destined for the direct protection of the leader were adopted and adapted by many societies over the centuries. The influence of the Praetorians extended beyond the borders of the empire, leaving an indelible mark on the modern conception of special forces and elite units. As we explore the history of the Praetorians, we glimpse not just an imperial guard but a force that shaped the narrative of loyalty, discipline, and the crucial role of special forces in maintaining power and stability. Let us continue our journey, where the Praetorians become guardians of a legacy that transcends the confines of Ancient Rome.

In Search of Origins

As we traverse the pages of history, from the origins of special forces to the legends of the Myrmidons and Praetorians, we delve into an immortal legacy of courage, discipline, and loyalty. The journey has taken us through battlefields and imperial palaces, revealing how the roots of these special forces permeate the essence of war and leadership.

Interwoven Lessons in the Tapestry of Time

In the early days, the need to face unique challenges generated the first seeds of special forces. Adaptation and innovation shaped exceptional warriors capable of transcending the limitations of conventional conflict. The Myrmidons embodied unyielding discipline, while the Praetorians became the supreme guardians of imperial power.

Discipline, Loyalty, and Resilience

The Myrmidons, led by Achilles, stood out not only for physical strength but for the discipline that sustained their effectiveness. The loyalty of the Praetorians, in turn, surpassed boundaries, establishing a direct connection between the protection of the emperor and the stability of the empire. In both cases, discipline and loyalty were the pillars that sustained special forces.

Enduring Impact on Military History

The legacy left by these mythical troops transcended eras, influencing the modern conception of special forces. Lessons learned in ancient battles of Troy and Roman palaces resonate in the corridors of modern training grounds. Discipline, loyalty, and the ability to face extraordinary challenges remain timeless values in contemporary special forces.

Exploring the Link between Past and Future

As we conclude this chapter, we look not only backward but to the bridge that connects the past to the future. The lessons of these mythical troops are beacons that illuminate the path to high-performance teams in contemporary management. Let us embark, then, on this journey in search of the link between ages, where ancient traditions intertwine with the challenges and opportunities of the modern world.

Chapter 2

"Forging the Elite: Lessons from the Masters of War"

The Schools of the Elite

As we enter the second chapter of our journey, we are led into the corridors of military elite schools. Here, not only are exceptional warriors shaped, but the lessons that permeate contemporary special forces are forged. Let's explore the backstage of military academies and training grounds that gave rise to some of the most formidable units in history.

The Rigor of the SAS: Forging the British Vanguard

From the North African Desert to the Mountains of Afghanistan

The UK's Special Air Service (SAS) emerges as an elite force known for its adaptability to any environment. Founded during World War II, the SAS played a crucial role in operations in the North African desert, conducting raids behind enemy lines. The versatility of their operations is evident in their rigorous training, including survival techniques, navigation, and specialized combat skills in different geographical contexts. SAS candidates undergo an extremely demanding selection known as the "SAS Selection Test" or "Fan Dance." This rigorous test, conducted in the Brecon Beacons mountains, challenges aspirants in terms of physical endurance, mental resilience, and navigation skills in rugged terrain.

The Art of Survival of the Navy SEALs:
From Water to Land

Amphibious Operations and Beyond

The United States Navy SEALs are known for their ability to transition fluidly between aquatic and terrestrial environments. Their training is extensive and diverse, including amphibious operations, combat diving, land navigation, and survival training in adverse conditions. SEAL candidates go through the feared and challenging BUD/S (Basic Underwater Demolition/SEAL) Training, which is one of the toughest military trainings in the world. During BUD/S, aspirants are tested in physical endurance, diving skills, open-water navigation, and special operations in different environments.

Spetsnaz: The Ferocity of the Russian Elite

From Urban Warfare Training to Frozen Borders

Russian special forces, known as Spetsnaz, are notable for their comprehensive approach, including urban operations, survival training in extreme climates, and infiltration skills. Originating from the Cold War, Spetsnaz is a Russian response to Western elite units. Spetsnaz training is intensive and diverse. They are trained in hand-to-hand combat, survival techniques, ambush operations, and infiltration methods. Additionally, they are prepared to operate in complex urban environments, making them a highly versatile force.

Lessons Forged in the Heat of Battle As we explore the various approaches of special forces around the world, we realize that, although tactics and environments vary, there is a constant: the need for versatility, resilience, and unwavering commitment to excellence. The training of these elite units not only forges exceptional warriors but also shapes the crucial lessons that will be explored on our path toward forming high-performance teams. In the next stage, we will delve into the key elements of the training of these units and discover how these lessons can be applied in contemporary management contexts.

Chapter 3

"Key Training Elements: Forging Cohesion and Resilience"

The Core of Training

As we progress on our journey, we delve into the core of special forces training. This chapter guides us through the key elements that forge not only skilled warriors but cohesive and resilient teams. From cohesion in operations to developing resilience in the face of adversity, we explore how these elements shape the character of special forces and, by extension, how they can be applied in contemporary management contexts.

Team Cohesion: The Unbreakable Link

Bonds That Do Not Break

Team cohesion is more than just teamwork; it is the construction of indestructible bonds among members. In a practical scenario, envision a special operations team carrying out a rescue mission in an urban environment. Each member has a specific role, from the leader coordinating the action to the communications specialist maintaining essential connectivity. The success of the mission depends on the unwavering trust that each member places in the others, reflecting the cohesion forged in training.

Cooperation Exercises

During these exercises, team members may encounter simulated challenges such as rescuing individuals in abandoned buildings or evacuating hostile areas. Every move is choreographed to promote cooperation and trust. These practical situations, often based on real experiences, allow the team to develop a deep understanding of individual capabilities, strengthening the bonds that form the backbone of cohesion.

Resilience Development: Facing Adversity with Steadfastness

Preparation for the Unexpected

Resilience is tested and cultivated in simulated situations that replicate the extremes of war and special missions. In a hypothetical scenario, imagine a special forces team facing a surprise counterattack while conducting a reconnaissance operation. Uncertainty, stress, and intense pressure simulate real-world conditions, challenging members to maintain focus and operational effectiveness.

Crisis Simulations Crisis simulations are vital for developing resilience. Team members may be subjected to complex scenarios, such as emergency evacuation under enemy fire or an infiltration mission in unknown terrain. These simulations not only test technical skills but also the ability to make quick and efficient decisions under pressure, building the resilience needed to face unexpected situations.

Adaptive Leadership: Guiding Amidst Complexity

The Leader's Role in Cohesion and Resilience Adaptive leadership is exemplified in practical situations where the team is confronted with unexpected challenges. For instance, picture a special operations team leader dealing with an unexpected communication failure during a mission. The leader's ability to adapt, reorganize the strategy, and keep the team focused is essential for mission success.

Extreme Condition Leadership Exercises

Specific exercises challenge leaders to guide in extreme conditions. This may include simulations of complex missions such as rescues in hostile environments or evacuations from combat areas. The leader's adaptability is constantly tested and refined in these situations, preparing them to lead effectively in any scenario.

The Symphony of Cohesion and Resilience

At the end of this chapter, we realize that cohesion and resilience are not just aspects of special forces training but an intricate symphony that echoes through each mission. The ability to work together, stand firm in adversity, and exhibit adaptive leadership are key elements that not only forge warriors but shape teams capable of overcoming the most formidable challenges. In the next stage, we will apply these lessons in the context of contemporary management, exploring how these elements can be incorporated to form high-performance teams in corporate environments.

Chapter 4

"Contextualization: Importance in Contemporary Management"

The Crucial Role of High-Performance Teams

In this chapter, we enter the realm of contemporary management, where the dynamics of organizations are in constant evolution. We will explore why high-performance teams have become an urgent necessity, highlighting their influence on innovation, organizational effectiveness, and the ability to face the fluid challenges of the modern corporate world.

The Era of Corporate Speed and Complexity

Challenges Requiring Agile Responses

In contemporary management, companies face increasingly dynamic and complex challenges. Rapid changes in markets, accelerated technological advancements, and globalization impose a constant demand for agile responses. High-performance teams emerge as essential catalysts for agility and adaptability, enabling organizations to navigate efficiently through a constantly changing business landscape.

Innovation and Creativity: Engines of Competitiveness

Competitive Advantage of Innovation

Contemporary management not only demands quick responses but also values innovation and creativity as pillars of competitive advantage. High-performance teams, by their collaborative and cohesive nature, become fertile ground for the flourishing of innovative ideas. By exploring the diversity of skills and perspectives, these teams become driving forces of creativity, crucial for maintaining competitiveness in saturated markets.

Organizational Efficiency and Achieving Ambitious Goals

Sustainable Long-Term Performance

Contemporary management focuses on operational efficiency and the achievement of ambitious goals. High-performance teams, with their ability to work synergistically, have a direct impact on organizational effectiveness. They not only deliver consistent results but also ensure that long-term goals are achieved sustainably, creating a solid foundation for continuous growth.

Adapting to Organizational Changes

Flexibility to Face Changes

Contemporary management is characterized by frequent organizational changes, whether in structure, culture, or work practices. High-performance teams demonstrate remarkable flexibility in adapting to these changes. Their cohesion and resilience become valuable assets, providing a smooth and effective transition during periods of organizational transformation.

The Imperative of High-Performance Teams

As we delve into the waters of contemporary management, it becomes clear that high-performance teams are not just desirable but imperative. Their ability to tackle agile challenges, drive innovation, ensure organizational efficiency, and adapt to constant changes ensures they are the fundamental cornerstone for the success of organizations in the modern era. In the next stage, we will connect these considerations to the training of special forces, exploring how the lessons learned in this context can be applied in the formation of high-performance teams in the contemporary corporate environment.

Chapter 5

"Challenges in Team Formation: Overcoming Obstacles Towards High Efficiency"

Navigating the Challenges of Team Formation

As we enter this chapter, we delve into the intrinsic challenges of forming highly effective teams. From managing diversity to overcoming geographical barriers, we will explore strategies to tackle these obstacles and build cohesive and productive teams.

Diversity and Collaboration: Strength or Challenge?

Building Bridges Across Differences

Diversity is a driving force but can also be a challenge. In contemporary corporate environments, teams are often composed of members with distinct experiences, skills, and perspectives. Effectively managing this diversity is crucial to fostering collaboration. Strategies include awareness programs, inclusion training, and creating spaces where diversity is celebrated and utilized as a catalyst for innovation.

Geographical Barriers: Overcoming Physical Distance

Connecting Minds Despite Miles

Teams geographically distributed face the challenge of effective communication and cohesion. Digital tools, such as video conferences and online collaborative platforms, have become crucial allies in overcoming these barriers. Strategies for managing virtual teams include establishing regular meeting schedules, promoting transparency in communication, and ensuring all members feel connected despite physical distance.

Interpersonal Conflicts: Turning Challenges into Opportunities

Building Resilience in Relationships

Interpersonal conflicts can arise in any team, but the key lies in the ability to turn these challenges into opportunities for growth. Strategies include promoting an open dialogue culture, clearly setting expectations, and implementing conflict resolution processes. In high-performance teams, conflicts are seen as opportunities for innovation and continuous improvement.

Organizational Changes: Adapting to Transformation

Flexibility in the Face of Changes

The speed of organizational changes can be an obstacle to forming high-performance teams. Strategies involve creating flexible structures that can adapt quickly to changes, providing continuous training to empower team members to face new challenges, and transparently communicating impending changes.

Turning Challenges into Competitive Advantages

At the end of this chapter, we realize that challenges in team formation are not insurmountable obstacles but opportunities for growth and strengthening. Carefully developed strategies not only overcome these challenges but transform them into competitive advantages. In the next stage, we will integrate these reflections with the teachings of special forces, exploring how the strategies used by these teams can be adapted and applied to overcome common challenges in forming high-performance teams in the contemporary corporate environment.

Chapter 6

"Effective Leadership: Inspiration and Motivation in Special Forces"

The Art of Leadership

In this chapter, we will delve into the world of effective leadership in special forces. We will analyze how leaders inspire and motivate their teams, highlighting principles transferable to everyday management. From cohesion to resilience, we will explore the characteristics that make special forces leaders notable examples of effective leadership.

Inspiration through Action: Leaders as Role Models

Exemplifying Values and Behaviors

Special forces leaders often lead by example. They not only articulate essential values but embody them in their daily actions. This principle can be transferred to everyday management, where corporate leaders demonstrating integrity, resilience, and work ethic inspire and motivate their teams.

Building Trust: The Foundation of Cohesion

Transparency and Trust Relationships

Trust is the glue that keeps teams together. Special forces leaders build trust through transparency, open communication, and creating an environment where team members feel safe to express their opinions. These principles are equally applicable in corporate management, where trust is fundamental to the smooth functioning of the team.

Motivation in Challenging Environments

Awakening Determination

Challenging environments are the norm for special forces, and leaders of these units are skilled in motivating their teams amid adversity. This same principle can be applied in management, where motivational leaders drive their teams to achieve ambitious goals even in challenging scenarios.

Clear and Effective Communication

Conveying Vision and Objectives

Special forces leaders are masters of clear and effective communication. They convey the mission's vision unequivocally and ensure that each team member understands their role. In corporate management, the ability to communicate objectives clearly and engagingly is essential to keeping the team aligned and motivated.

Transferable Principles for Leadership

In concluding this chapter, we recognize that effective leadership in special forces is not an isolated phenomenon but a set of transferable principles for everyday management. From inspiring by example to building trust and motivating in challenging environments, special forces leaders provide an inspiring model for leaders in all contexts. In the next stage, we will connect these lessons to high-performance team training, exploring how the leadership principles of special forces can be integrated into the formation of corporate leaders.

Chapter 7

"Clear Communication: Unveiling the Importance in High-Pressure Environments"

The Vital Role of Clear Communication

In this chapter, we will delve into the importance of clear communication in high-pressure environments, such as those found in special forces. We will explore strategies for direct and effective communication and how these lessons can be practically applied in business communication, where clarity is a pillar for success.

The Need for Clarity in Critical Environments

Reducing Noise in Decisive Moments

In high-pressure environments, clear communication is essential to avoid misunderstandings and minimize the risk of errors. Special forces leaders ensure that information is conveyed directly and understandably. In business communication, this approach is equally crucial, especially in critical moments, to ensure that messages are received and understood as intended.

The Power of Concise Communication Conveying Information Efficiently

In critical missions, every word counts. Communication in special forces is characterized by conciseness and clarity, ensuring that essential information is transmitted efficiently. In the corporate world, the ability to communicate concisely is a valuable tool, allowing for faster and more effective exchange of information, especially in fast decision-making situations.

Adapting the Message to the Audience Understanding Relevance for Different Audiences

Special forces leaders adapt their communication to meet the specific needs of different audiences. This approach is crucial in the business world, where effective communication requires an understanding of the characteristics and needs of various stakeholders. Adapting the message to the target audience is essential to ensure that the information is relevant and impactful.

Transparency and Trust in Communication Building a Trust Foundation

In high-pressure environments, transparency is a cornerstone of effective communication. Special forces leaders share information openly to build trust among team members. This practice is transferable to the business environment, where transparent communication strengthens the bonds between leaders and their teams, creating a solid foundation of trust.

Applying the Lessons of Clear Communication in Business

In concluding this chapter, we understand that clear communication is not only a necessity in high-pressure environments but a transferable skill with a significant impact on business. Clarity in communication is a powerful tool to avoid misunderstandings, streamline processes, and build trust—essential elements for success in any endeavor. In the next stage, we will connect these clear communication practices to high-performance team training, exploring how communication clarity can be integrated to strengthen team effectiveness and cohesion.

Chapter 8

"Resilience and Adaptation: Navigating Unpredictable Situations"

The Need for Resilience and Adaptation

In this chapter, we will explore how teams deal with unpredictable situations, emphasizing the importance of resilience and adaptation. Special forces provide fertile ground for learning how to face the unexpected, and the lessons drawn will be applied to illustrate the relevance of these principles in organizations.

Resilience as the Pillar of Mental Strength Facing Challenges Without Breaking

In unpredictable situations, resilience is a fundamental pillar to maintain mental stability. Special forces members are trained to face extreme challenges without breaking, maintaining focus and operational effectiveness. This resilient mindset is transferable to organizations, where the ability to overcome adversities without losing direction is vital for long-term success.

Continuous Adaptation to Changes

Flexibility in the Face of Uncertainty

Unpredictable situations often demand continuous adaptation. Special forces teams are notable for their ability to adjust quickly to changes in scenario, strategy, or mission. Flexibility in the face of uncertainty is a valuable lesson for organizations, encouraging a culture that values continuous adaptation as a strategy for facing unexpected challenges.

Iterative Learning from Experiences

Growing with Each Challenge

In special forces, each mission is an opportunity for learning. Teams review and refine their approaches after each experience, using iterative learning to become more effective. In organizations, applying a mindset of continuous learning allows teams to grow with each challenge, turning adverse experiences into opportunities for improvement.

Building High-Performance Teams through Adversity

Strengthening Bonds in Tough Times

Unpredictable situations can test team cohesion. However, in special forces, adversity often strengthens the bonds among members. In organizations, the ability to build high-performance teams amid adversity is a strategic advantage, allowing team cohesion to be reinforced even in the face of unforeseen challenges.

Resilience and Adaptation as Long-Term Strategies

In concluding this chapter, we recognize that resilience and adaptation are not merely temporary responses to unpredictable situations but long-term strategies for facing constantly evolving challenges. The lessons learned from special forces offer valuable insights into building organizations that not only survive but thrive in the unexpected. In the next stage, we will integrate these resilience and adaptation practices into high-performance team training, exploring how these principles can be incorporated to strengthen teams' ability to face the unexpected.

Chapter 9

"Intensive Training: Forging Individual and Collective Skills"

The Importance of Rigorous Training

In this chapter, we will delve into the role of intensive training in building individual and collective skills. Inspired by the demanding training of special forces, we will explore how similar approaches can be applied to continuous professional development, both at the individual and collective levels.

Individual Development Through Personal Challenge

Overcoming Personal Limits

Intensive training in special forces challenges individual limits, forcing members to overcome physical and mental obstacles. This approach is transferable to professional development, where personal challenges stimulate individual growth. By facing challenging tasks, professionals can develop specific skills and strengthen resilience.

Realistic Simulations for Team Cohesion

Forging Lasting Bonds

Intensive training in special forces often includes realistic simulations of combat situations. These simulations not only enhance technical skills but also strengthen team cohesion. In organizations, realistic corporate simulations can be used to improve collaboration, communication, and problem-solving, creating more cohesive and effective teams.

Continuous Training Cycles for Skill Updates

Constant Evolution

Special forces members participate in continuous training cycles to stay updated and adapt to changes in the operational environment. This approach is applicable to professional development, where continuous learning and skill updates are essential to remain relevant in dynamic corporate environments.

Mentoring and Intergenerational Learning

Knowledge Transmission

In special forces, mentoring plays a crucial role in transmitting knowledge and experience. In organizations, creating mentoring programs promotes the transfer of skills and knowledge between generations of professionals, contributing to the continuous development of the team.

Cultivating a Culture of Continuous Development

By concluding this chapter, we understand that intensive training is not just an isolated event but a mindset that permeates the entire organizational culture. By applying similar approaches to professional development, we cultivate a culture of continuous learning and evolution, preparing individuals and teams to face constantly changing challenges and opportunities. In the next stage, we will explore how to incorporate this culture of continuous development into team training, ensuring that the pursuit of excellence is a constant journey.

Chapter 10

"Team Culture: Building Foundations for High Performance"

The Importance of Team Culture

In this chapter, we will explore how to create and maintain a cohesive culture that fosters trust and collaboration—essential elements for the success of high-performance teams. Inspired by the dynamics of special forces, we will analyze how these principles can be applied in corporate environments to strengthen the foundations of a team.

Building Trust: The Foundation of Team Culture

Fostering Trust Relationships

Trust is a fundamental pillar in high-performance teams. In special forces, trust is cultivated through shared experiences, transparency, and mutual support. In organizations, fostering trust relationships requires authentic leadership, open communication, and the promotion of an environment where team members feel safe to express ideas and concerns.

Collaboration as a Catalyst for Innovation

Harnessing Collective Intelligence

High-performance teams in special forces value collaboration as a source of innovation. The diversity of skills and perspectives is explored to find creative solutions. In organizations, promoting collaboration means creating spaces for idea-sharing, recognizing the importance of collective intelligence in solving complex problems.

Sharing Goals and a Common Vision

Alignment of Purpose

In special forces teams, each member clearly understands the goals and vision of the mission. This promotes alignment of purpose, essential for team cohesion. Similarly, in organizations, sharing goals and a common vision are crucial to ensure that all team members are working in the same direction.

Recognition and Celebration of Collective Achievements

Strengthening Team Identity

Celebrating collective achievements strengthens the team's identity. In special forces, recognition is an integral part of the culture. In organizations, recognizing and celebrating collective achievements creates a positive environment, encouraging commitment and dedication from team members.

Sustaining a High-Performance Culture

By concluding this chapter, we understand that team culture is not just a superficial aspect but a set of values and practices that permeate the entire organization. Inspired by the principles of special forces, we can shape a culture that not only promotes high performance but also creates an environment where team members feel valued and motivated. In the next stage, we will explore how to incorporate these cultural elements into team training, ensuring that cohesion and high performance are rooted in the team's identity.

Chapter 11

"Quick Decision-Making: Strategies for High-Pressure Environments"

In this chapter, we will delve into how teams handle crucial decisions in critical moments, exploring strategies applicable to managing corporate crises. Inspired by the agility of special forces, we will analyze how these strategies can be incorporated to ensure quick and effective decision-making in high-pressure environments.

Clarity of Purpose in Decision-Making

Mission Focus

In critical moments, clarity of purpose is essential for quick decision-making. In special forces, mission focus guides choices in high-pressure environments. Similarly, in corporate crises, a clear definition of objectives allows for decision-making aligned with organizational goals.

Rapid Analysis of Relevant Information

Efficiency in Data Assessment

Special forces teams are trained to quickly analyze relevant information and make informed decisions. In organizations, the ability to assess data efficiently is crucial. Strategies such as implementing agile information systems and promoting a culture of critical analysis facilitate decision-making based on accurate information.

Flexibility to Change Course Quickly

Adaptation to Evolving Scenarios

In high-pressure environments, the ability to change course quickly is an advantage. Special forces are known for their flexibility in adapting to evolving scenarios. Similarly, in managing corporate crises, flexibility is crucial. Agile strategies and well-developed contingency plans enable a rapid response to unexpected changes.

Distribution of Authority and Responsibility

Empowering Decision-Making

In special forces, the distribution of authority allows team members to make crucial decisions in their areas of expertise. In organizations, effective delegation of responsibilities and authority is fundamental for quick decision-making. Empowering team members to act swiftly in their areas of competence contributes to an agile response in critical situations.

Integrated Strategies for Decision-Making Under Pressure

By concluding this chapter, we understand that quick decision-making is a critical skill in high-pressure environments, whether on the battlefield or in business. By integrating strategies inspired by special forces, organizations can enhance their ability to make agile and effective decisions in crucial moments. In the next stage, we will explore how to incorporate these strategies into team training, ensuring that decision-making under pressure is a skill cultivated and continuously refined.

Chapter 12

Integrated Training for High-Performance Teams

In this phase, we will advance to integrated training for high-performance teams, incorporating the principles and strategies explored in the previous chapters. The goal is to provide a practical experience that strengthens team cohesion, develops individual and collective skills, and promotes a culture of high performance.

Simulations of Missions and Practical Exercises:

- Develop realistic simulations that challenge teams to apply the principles learned in practical situations.

- Integrate specific exercises to promote clear communication, quick decision-making, and collaborative work under pressure.

Training Focused on Individual and Collective Skills:

- Implement intensive training programs that focus on the continuous development of individual skills, such as leadership, resilience, and adaptability.

- Include training that strengthens collective skills, such as teamwork, collaboration, and group problem-solving.

Mentoring and Intergenerational Learning:

- Establish mentoring programs that facilitate the transfer of knowledge between more experienced members and new team members.

- Encourage the exchange of experiences and perspectives, promoting an environment of continuous learning.

Fostering a Team Culture:

- Conduct activities that build trust, such as group dynamics and team-building exercises.

- Promote collaboration and goal sharing through workshops and events emphasizing the importance of a common vision.

Training in Decision-Making Under Pressure:

- Simulate business crisis situations for teams to practice quick and effective decision-making.

- Integrate exercises that emphasize the rapid analysis of relevant information and flexibility to adapt to evolving scenarios.

Continuous Assessment and Constructive Feedback:

- Implement continuous assessment systems to monitor individual and team progress.

- Provide constructive feedback to encourage continuous improvement and practical application of learned concepts.

This stage will not only consolidate the acquired knowledge but also allow the team to develop the skills and attitudes necessary to face real challenges. By integrating high-performance team training holistically, organizations will be better prepared to achieve operational excellence and stand out in dynamic environments.

Chapter 13

Practical Application in Business Scenarios

In this phase, we will focus our efforts on the practical application of the knowledge and skills acquired in real business scenarios. The focus will be on adapting the principles learned to address specific challenges within the organization. We will address:

Mapping Organizational Challenges:

- Identify specific challenges faced by the organization.

- Analyze how the learned strategies and principles can be applied to overcome these challenges.

Development of Action Plans:

- Develop action plans tailored to identified challenges.

- Integrate leadership, teamwork, decision-making, and resilience concepts into the plans.

Implementation in Work Environments:

- Gradually introduce practices and changes derived from training into daily operations.

- Monitor the acceptance and effectiveness of the implemented changes.

Impact Assessment:

- Measure the impact of adaptations and changes in the work environment.

- Collect feedback from employees to evaluate the effectiveness of implemented initiatives.

Iteration and Continuous Improvement:

- Identify areas for improvement based on impact assessment.

- Iterate on action plans to optimize the practical application of learned principles.

Development of a Lasting Organizational Culture:

- Foster a culture that values continuous learning, innovation, and the pursuit of excellence.

- Integrate teamwork, leadership, and resilience principles into the organizational identity

This topic aims to ensure that the lessons learned during training translate into tangible improvements in organizational processes and results. By applying knowledge in an adapted and strategic manner, the team will be prepared to face specific challenges in the business environment, promoting a culture of high performance and excellence.

Chapter 14

Continuous Learning and Organizational Evolution

In this phase, we will focus our efforts on establishing practices for continuous learning and promoting the constant evolution of the organization. This topic will address:

Creation of Professional Development Programs:

- Implement continuous training and development programs for all levels of the organization.

- Include workshops, seminars, and courses addressing topics relevant to the evolving needs of the organization.

Facilitation of Knowledge Sharing:

- Establish platforms and practices that facilitate efficient knowledge sharing among team members.

- Encourage the creation of communities of practice for the exchange of experiences and insights.

Integration of New Organizational Practices:

- Continuously assess industry trends and best practices.

- Agilely and effectively integrate new approaches and technologies that can benefit the organization.

Feedback and Continuous Evaluation:

- Establish a robust feedback system involving all members of the organization.

- Use regular assessments to identify areas for improvement and growth opportunities.

Culture of Innovation and Experimentation:

- Promote a culture that encourages innovation and experimentation.

- Encourage employees to seek creative solutions to organizational challenges.

Exemplary Leadership:

- Develop leadership programs that empower leaders to promote a culture of continuous learning.

- Model active learning behavior, demonstrating the importance of constant growth.

Adaptation to External Changes:

- Continuously monitor the external environment for changes in the market, technology, and regulations.

- Develop agile strategies to proactively adapt to these changes.

This topic aims to establish a mindset of continuous learning and ensure that the organization is always adapting and evolving. By prioritizing professional development, innovation, and adaptation to changes, the organization will be better positioned to face the constantly evolving challenges of the business environment.

Chapter 15

Measurement of Results and Impact Assessment

In this stage, we will focus on measuring results and assessing the impact of implemented initiatives. This will ensure that the organization has a clear understanding of how the changes have affected its objectives and where improvements can be made. We will address:

Definition of Key Performance Indicators (KPIs):

- Identify and establish KPIs aligned with the organization's strategic objectives.

- Include indicators that reflect the effectiveness of high-performance practices and continuous learning.

Data Collection:

- Implement efficient systems for collecting data related to defined KPIs.

- Use analysis tools and metrics to gain detailed insights.

Results Analysis:

- Conduct a detailed analysis of the collected data to assess the organization's performance.

- Compare the obtained results with established goals.

Employee Feedback:

- Collect feedback from employees on the implemented changes.

- Conduct surveys, interviews, or focus groups to understand the team's perception and experience.

Adjustments and Optimizations:

- Based on results analysis and employee feedback, make adjustments to implemented practices and strategies.

- Seek continuous optimizations to improve the effectiveness of initiatives.

Impact Report:

- Develop a comprehensive report highlighting the achieved results and noticeable changes.

- Share this information with the entire organization to promote transparency and recognition of efforts.

Creation of a Continuous Assessment Cycle:

- Establish a continuous cycle of assessment and adjustment based on results and evolving organizational needs.

- Integrate result measurement as an integral part of the organizational culture.

  This topic aims to ensure that the organization is always aligned with its objectives, using concrete data to guide future decisions and promote a culture of continuous improvement.

Chapter 16

Sustainment and Continuity

In this phase, we will address strategies to sustain the gains achieved and maintain continuous evolution. The continuity of high-performance and continuous learning practices requires a long-term commitment. We will cover:

Creation of Support Structures:

• Establishment of organizational structures that support and promote high-performance practices.

• Assignment of specific responsibilities to ensure the continuity of initiatives.

Development of Leaders as Mentors:

• Empowering leaders to act as mentors, promoting a culture of continuous learning.

• Encouraging the transmission of knowledge and experience between leaders and team members.

Incorporation into Human Resources Processes:

• Integration of high-performance practices into recruitment, training, and human resources development processes.

• Ensuring that new team members align with the established organizational culture.

Recognition and Rewards Programs:

• Implementation of programs that recognize and reward contributions to the high-performance and continuous learning culture.

• Inclusion of incentives that promote individual and team excellence.

Continuous Communication:

• Maintaining transparent communication about the organization's progress and objectives.

• Holding regular meetings to align the team and provide updates on future initiatives.

Organizational Climate Monitoring:

• Implementation of organizational climate monitoring tools to identify any emerging challenges.

• Proactive intervention in issues that may impact organizational culture.

Periodic Effectiveness Evaluation:

• Conducting periodic evaluations to measure the effectiveness of sustainability practices.

• Constant adjustment of strategies based on the results of these assessments. This topic aims to ensure that high-performance and continuous learning practices become an intrinsic part of the organizational culture, ensuring the sustainability of efforts and continuous evolution over time.

Chapter 17

Expansion and Replication of the Model

In this phase, we will explore how to successfully expand and replicate the high-performance and continuous learning team model to other areas or units of the organization. We will cover:

Identification of Expansion Opportunities:

• Evaluation of areas or departments that would benefit from implementing the model.

• Identification of specific opportunities to replicate successful practices.

Adaptation of the Model for Various Contexts:

• Modification and adaptation of the model to meet the needs and peculiarities of different areas or units.

• Consideration of cultural and operational nuances in each context.

Training and Empowerment:

• Development of training programs to introduce the model's principles to new teams.

• Empowerment of leaders and team members to ensure effective implementation.

Sharing Successful Experiences:

• Creation of communication channels to share experiences and learnings among different areas.

• Promotion of a cohesive and interconnected organizational culture.

Iterative Feedback:

• Continuous collection of feedback during expansion to identify areas for improvement.

• Constant adjustment of the model based on received feedback.

Performance Indicator Monitoring:

• Establishment of specific performance indicators for each area.

• Continuous monitoring to assess the impact and effectiveness of the expanded model.

Recognition and Celebration of Achievements:

• Public recognition of teams that adopt and succeed with the model.

• Celebration of individual and collective achievements through implementation. This phase aims to ensure that the success of the model is effectively replicated in different parts of the organization, promoting a unified culture of high performance and continuous learning.

Chapter 18

Adaptation to Future Challenges and Continuous Innovation

In this stage, we will address how the organization can adapt to future challenges and maintain a mindset of continuous innovation. This involves anticipating changes in the business environment and preparing to evolve according to emerging demands. We will cover:

Analysis of Trends and Changes in the Business Environment:

• Constant monitoring of trends and changes in the market and industry.

• Analysis of how these changes may impact the organization and its practices.

Fostering a Culture of Innovation:

• Encouragement of generating innovative ideas at all levels of the organization. • Creation of spaces for experimentation and implementation of new approaches.

Development of Adaptation Capabilities:

• Promotion of training and programs that develop the team's ability to adapt quickly to changes.

• Encouragement of flexibility and resilience in the face of unforeseen challenges.

Establishment of Strategic Partnerships:

• Exploration of strategic partnerships that can bring new perspectives and resources to the organization.

• Collaboration with other companies, academic institutions, and organizations to drive innovation.

Investment in Emerging Technologies:

• Evaluation and implementation of emerging technologies that can improve organizational efficiency and effectiveness.

• Integration of technological solutions aligned with the organization's goals.

Promotion of Continuous Learning:

• Continuation of training and development programs to keep the team updated.

• Active support for the constant pursuit of new knowledge and relevant skills.

Risk Assessment and Contingency Preparation:

• Proactive identification of potential risks and vulnerabilities.

• Development of contingency plans to deal with adverse situations. This topic aims to ensure that the organization is prepared to face future challenges, maintaining a culture of innovation and continuous learning that positions it resiliently in the market.

Chapter 19

Legacy and Sustainable Impact

In this phase, we will explore how to consolidate the legacy of high-performance and continuous learning practices, ensuring sustainable long-term impact. This involves creating a solid foundation that endures even after changes in leadership or the organizational environment. We will cover:

Incorporation into Organizational Values:

• Ensuring that high-performance and continuous learning principles are incorporated into the organization's core values.

• Creating a lasting commitment to these principles.

Documentation and Knowledge Transmission:

• Creation of manuals, documents, and resources capturing key practices and learnings from the journey.

• Establishment of processes to transmit this knowledge to new generations of employees.

Succession Programs:

• Development of succession programs that identify and prepare leaders to take on key roles.

• Gradual transfer of responsibilities and knowledge to ensure a smooth transition.

Long-Term Metrics:

• Establishment of long-term metrics assessing the ongoing impact of implemented practices.

• Monitoring organizational legacy over time.

Recognition of Individual Contributions:

• Recognition and celebration of individual contributions to the development of the high-performance culture.

• Creation of awards or honors highlighting commitment and dedication.

Engagement of the Organizational Community:

• Promotion of involvement and active participation of all members of the organizational community in preserving the culture.

• Encouragement of the continued commitment to established principles.

Periodic Legacy Evaluation:

• Conducting periodic evaluations to check the effectiveness of legacy preservation strategies.

• Constant adjustment of approaches based on the results of these evaluations.

This topic aims to ensure that the impact of high-performance and continuous learning practices is lasting, forming a legacy that positively contributes to the organization's future.

Chapter 20

Reflection and Constant Renewal

In this phase, we will explore the importance of constant reflection and renewal to maintain the vitality of the high-performance and continuous learning culture. This includes practices that allow the organization to adapt to new contexts and challenges. We will cover:

Assessment of Continuous Relevance:

• Conducting periodic assessments to determine the continuous relevance of high-performance principles.

• Adaptation and adjustment as the needs of the business environment evolve.

Discussion Forums and Feedback:

• Establishment of regular forums for open discussion and feedback collection.

• Encouragement of the expression of innovative ideas and suggestions for improvement.

Internal Innovation Programs:

• Implementation of programs that encourage internal innovation.

• Creation of channels for employees to share disruptive ideas.

Development of New Methodologies:

• Exploration of new methodologies and approaches to high performance.

• Integration of innovative practices aligned with the organization's vision and mission.

Encouragement of Continuous Learning:

• Promotion of a culture that values continuous learning.

• Active support for the development of relevant skills for emerging challenges.

Flexibility in Organizational Practices:

• Adoption of a flexible approach to organizational practices.

• Ability to adjust policies and procedures as necessary.

Celebrating Achievements and Milestones:

• Recognition and celebration of significant achievements along the way.

• Positive reinforcement to maintain team engagement and enthusiasm.

This topic emphasizes the importance of constant reflection, adaptation, and continuous renewal to ensure that the high-performance culture remains dynamic and aligned with the organization's constantly evolving goals.

Chapter 21

The Organizational Transformation Journey

In this final phase, we will address the organizational transformation journey as a whole, highlighting key points and learnings throughout the process. This will include:

Transformation Narrative:

- Creating a narrative that tells the story of organizational transformation.
- Highlighting milestones, challenges overcome, and successes along the journey.

Impact on Organizational Results

- Evaluating the impact of transformation on financial, operational, and customer satisfaction results.
- Comparing metrics before and after the implementation of high-performance and continuous learning practices.

Testimonials and Success Stories:

- Collecting testimonials from employees who experienced the transformation.
- Showcasing success stories that illustrate the effectiveness of implemented practices.

Lessons Learned:

- Identifying and documenting lessons learned throughout the journey.
- Reflecting on challenges overcome and how these challenges contributed to organizational growth.

Recognition and Appreciation:

- Recognizing and expressing gratitude to everyone involved in the transformation.
- Highlighting collective effort and individual dedication.

Vision for the Future:

- Presenting the vision for the organization's future after transformation.
- Defining goals and aspirations that continue to drive growth and innovation.

Continuous Engagement:

- Establishing strategies to maintain team engagement and motivation.
- Encouraging ongoing commitment to a culture of high performance and continuous learning. This phase concludes the journey, providing a comprehensive view of organizational transformation. It emphasizes not only tangible results but also the impact on people and the organization's culture, solidifying transformation as an integral part of the identity and future of the organization.

Chapter 22

After completing the organizational transformation journey, the next step would be to focus on the continuous implementation of established practices, monitoring results, and constantly adapting to changes in the business environment. This may involve:

Continuous Implementation:

- Ensuring that high-performance and continuous learning practices are an integral part of daily processes.
- Ensuring that new team members are integrated into the organizational culture from the outset.

Monitoring Key Indicators:

- Continuing to monitor key performance indicators established during the transformation.
- Conducting regular assessments to ensure that the organization is on the right track toward its goals.

Continuous Improvement:

- Identifying improvement opportunities based on continuous feedback and performance evaluations.
- Iterating on existing practices to ensure they remain aligned with organizational needs and goals.

Continuous Professional Development:

- Maintaining professional development programs to ensure the team is constantly improving their skills.

- Exploring new trends and relevant technologies for the industry.

Creating a Culture of Innovation:

- Continuing to promote a culture of innovation, encouraging experimentation, and seeking creative solutions.
- Exploring opportunities to implement emerging technologies and innovative practices.

Community Engagement:

- Fostering continuous engagement of the organizational community in preserving and evolving the established culture.
- Encouraging collaboration and knowledge sharing among team members.

Adapting to External Changes:

- Remaining vigilant to changes in the external environment that may impact the organization.
- Developing agile strategies to proactively adapt to these changes. This post-transformation phase is marked by the consolidation of gains and the continuous pursuit of organizational excellence. Remaining agile, adaptable, and committed to continuous learning is essential to ensure that the organization continues to evolve and excel in a dynamic business environment.

Chapter 23

After the continuous implementation of established practices and the consolidation of gains, the cycle of organizational improvement and evolution can continue with various approaches:

Innovation and Cutting-Edge Research:

- Investing in research and development programs to stay at the forefront of innovation.
- Exploring new technologies, methods, and strategies that can provide competitive advantages.

Expansion into New Markets or Sectors:

- Evaluating opportunities for expansion into new markets or sectors.
- Applying high-performance and continuous learning practices in different contexts and adapting as necessary.

Strategic Partnerships and Mergers:

- Seeking strategic partnerships and mergers that can strengthen the organization's position in the market.
- Integrating new cultural elements and practices, leveraging the best from each entity.

Sustainability and Social Responsibility:

- Incorporating sustainable practices and social responsibility into the organization's operations.

- Demonstrating a continuous commitment to ethics, environmental responsibility, and social responsibility.

Leadership Development and Succession:

- Continuing to invest in leadership development and succession programs.
- Ensuring strong leadership prepared to take on strategic roles as the organization evolves.

Adoption of Innovative Business Models:

- Exploring new business models that can bring operational efficiencies and greater value to customers.
- Staying attentive to changes in customer expectations and market trends.

Culture of Continuous Improvement:

- Establishing an organizational culture that values continuous improvement in all aspects.
- Encouraging bottom-up innovation, where ideas and suggestions from employees are valued.

This post-continuous implementation phase represents a constant cycle of assessment, adaptation, and growth. By maintaining an agile mindset, being oriented toward continuous learning, and being open to innovation, the organization will be well-positioned to face future challenges and thrive in a dynamic business environment.

Chapter 24

The Vital Role of Managers in Inspiring and Motivating Teams

In the vast territory of management, managers are the architects who shape the culture and performance of teams. This chapter aims to explore the crucial role played by managers in inspiring and motivating teams, revealing leadership practices that transcend mere supervision.

Section 1: Inspiring Through Vision:

Vision is the compass that guides a team toward its goals. In this section, we will examine how managers can articulate a compelling vision, instilling a sense of purpose that goes beyond daily tasks. Through case studies and practical examples, we will highlight how inspiring leaders paint a convincing picture of the future, aligning the team with a narrative that goes beyond numbers and targets.

Section 2: Motivation Beyond Financial Incentives:

If vision is the compass, motivation is the fuel that drives the journey. Here, we will explore innovative approaches to motivate teams, going beyond traditional financial incentives. We will analyze how visionary managers apply recognition, professional development, and a positive work environment to nurture the intrinsic passion of team members.

Section 3: Inspiring Communication:

Effective communication is the key to unlocking understanding and trust within the team. We will investigate how managers can enhance their communication skills to inspire and motivate. From the art of storytelling to the importance of active listening, this section will provide practical tools for managers to cultivate an open and inspiring communication environment.

Section 4: Developing a Recognition Culture:

Recognition is a powerful driving force. In this section, we will examine how managers can develop a culture of recognition that celebrates achievements, big or small. Through tangible strategies and recognition programs, managers can strengthen the bond among team members and promote a sense of belonging and accomplishment.

Section 5: Authentic Leadership:

Authenticity is the glue that binds leaders and teams. We will address the importance of authentic leadership, highlighting how managers can be models of integrity and transparency. We will investigate case studies of authentic leaders who inspired trust and built lasting relationships with their teams.

As we explore the role of managers in inspiring and motivating teams, it becomes evident that true leadership transcends goal fulfillment. Visionary managers not only coordinate tasks but cultivate an environment that nurtures human potential. This chapter will be a compass for managers, guiding them in building motivated and inspired teams capable of facing challenges with resilience and achieving remarkable accomplishments.

Chapter 25

Talent Development - A Strategic Approach Inspired by Special Forces Intensive Training

In the realm of special forces, where excellence is not just desired but vital, training emerges as the backbone of success. This chapter delves into the heart of talent development in organizations, a journey inspired by the meticulous and intensive approach adopted by special forces. By unraveling effective strategies, we seek not only to propel the continuous growth of team members but also to align ourselves with the rigorous training that characterizes elite units.

Section 1: Identifying Potential:

Like talent archaeologists, managers can unearth latent skills that may not be apparent at first glance. In this section, we explore methods for potential identification, emphasizing the importance of strategic assessments and continuous feedback. By inspiring managers to recognize and nurture skills, we unlock the true potential of each team member.

Section 2: Personalized Development:

Just as special forces tailor training to individual skills, managers can create customized programs that cater to the unique needs of each team member. From mentorships to specialized courses, this section serves as a practical guide for personalized development, catalyzing professional and personal growth.

Section 3: The Importance of Constructive Feedback:

Feedback is the compass that guides the development journey. In this section, we analyze the importance of constructive feedback, highlighting how managers can offer effective guidance that inspires growth. Case studies illustrate how feedback becomes a powerful tool for shaping skills and enhancing performance.

Section 4: Developing Technical and Behavioral Skills:

Just as special forces balance technical and behavioral skills, this section addresses the development of both dimensions. We explore strategies to enhance specific technical skills related to team functions while emphasizing the development of behavioral skills such as leadership, resilience, and teamwork.

Section 5: Continuing Education Programs:

Special forces are always learning, always improving. In this section, we examine how managers can implement continuing education programs, promoting constant learning. From online courses to partnerships with educational institutions, this section offers insights into creating a development culture that transcends conventional boundaries.

By navigating the terrain of talent development, inspired by the intense training of special forces, this chapter is not just an exploration but a compass for managers seeking to build resilient and skilled teams. Continuous development is not just a strategy; it's a commitment to excellence. May these strategies inspire managers to cultivate an environment where each team member is encouraged to evolve continually, thus contributing to the lasting success of the organization.

Chapter 26

Creating a Conducive Environment - Nurturing Grounds for the Flourishing of High-Performance Teams

In this chapter, we delve into the essence of leadership, exploring how managers can be architects of an environment conducive to the flourishing of high-performance teams. Inspired by the principles of special forces, we immerse ourselves in creating fertile ground where excellence not only thrives but becomes inevitable.

Section 1: Cultivating Trust:

Trust is the foundation upon which robust teams are built. In this section, we will examine strategies for managers to cultivate trust within the team. We will address transparency, consistency, and accountability as key elements to nurture an environment where each team member feels safe to contribute fully.

Section 2: Fostering Collaboration:

The flourishing of high-performance teams depends on effective collaboration. Here, we explore how managers can foster a collaborative culture, encouraging the exchange of ideas and synergy. Case studies will highlight successful initiatives that promoted collaboration, transcending hierarchical barriers.

Section 3: Flexibility and Innovation:

Conducive environments are not static; they adapt and innovate. We will analyze how managers can incorporate flexibility into processes and promote an innovative mindset. Practical examples will illustrate how agility becomes a catalyst for the flourishing of innovative ideas and effective problem-solving.

Section 4: Recognizing and Celebrating Success:

Celebrating achievements is vital to maintaining positive momentum. In this section, we explore how managers can recognize and celebrate individual and collective success. Recognition strategies, from simple praises to more elaborate programs, will be discussed as tools to strengthen the sense of accomplishment and belonging.

Section 5: Managing Conflicts Constructively:

In any team, conflicts are inevitable. However, how they are managed can determine the team's destiny. We will analyze strategies for managers to manage conflicts constructively, transforming challenges into opportunities for learning and growth.

This chapter is an invitation for managers to become architects of conducive environments, where teams not only exist but thrive. By cultivating trust, fostering collaboration, promoting flexibility, celebrating success, and managing conflicts constructively, managers become leaders who not only lead but create fertile grounds for the lasting flourishing of high-performance teams. May this guide inspire managers to build not only teams but ecosystems where excellence is the norm, and success is a continuous journey.

Conclusion

Beyond the Frontiers of Organizational Transformation

Throughout this writing journey, we delved into the depths of organizational transformation, exploring the intricate connections between effective management, high-performance teams, and the invaluable lessons from special forces. Our initial goal of uncovering a path to build exceptional teams expanded to embrace a holistic view of contemporary management.

We began by contextualizing the vital importance of high-performance teams in modern management, revealing pressing challenges in forming these teams and outlining the crucial role of managers. In a unique synthesis, we united the legendary tradition of special forces, from the ancient Mirmidons to modern Navy SEALs and Spetsnaz, with the fundamentals of effective management.

The title "Mission Given, Mission Accomplished" encapsulates the essence of our exploration. This bold title is not just a call to action but an invitation to transcend conventional boundaries of management and leadership.

By delving into the legendary origins of special forces, from the Mirmidons in ancient Greece to the Pretorians of Rome, we witnessed tireless discipline in the Trojan

War and unwavering loyalty to the Roman Emperor. These stories, interwoven with modern principles of special forces, served as pillars to build our understanding of truly exceptional teams.

We explored the importance in contemporary management, demystified challenges in forming high-performance teams, and highlighted the vital responsibility of managers. Each chapter was a journey, a bridge between the past and present, connecting timeless lessons from special forces with the urgent needs of modern organizations.

From the discipline instilled by the Mirmidons to the Roman elite of the Pretorians, and from the arid environments of Navy SEALs to the stealthy operations of Spetsnaz, each narrative contributed to a cohesive mosaic of learning. These lessons transcended battlefields to illuminate corporate hallways, offering valuable principles to build teams that not only face challenges but thrive in the face of them.

In addressing challenges in team formation, we tackled topics such as diversity, communication, and resilience. Each topic was a piece in the management puzzle, emphasizing the importance of inspiring leaders, clear communication, resilience, and quick decision-making. We learned that, like special forces, high-performance teams require a cohesive culture, intense training, and a decisive approach in the face of uncertainty.

We moved beyond battlefields and boardrooms to explore the universe of special forces, from the call of the Mirmidons to the Roman vanguard of the Pretorians, incorporating modern tactics of Navy SEALs and Spetsnaz. Each narrative brought timeless lessons about discipline, loyalty, innovation, and leadership that echoed in boardrooms and corporate corridors.

The project overview, with outlined chapters, established the framework for our exploration. Each chapter became a portal to a new understanding, an invitation to apply the principles learned and transform not only teams but the entire organizational culture.

Reflecting on the early steps of special forces revealed a universal truth: emergencies demand extraordinary responses. The Mirmidons, with their unwavering discipline in the Trojan War, and the Pretorians, as guardians of the Roman Emperor, showed us that the need for special forces arose from the most crucial circumstances.

By delving into the stories of the Mirmidons, we understood discipline as the backbone of operational excellence. The Roman vanguard of the Pretorians, as guardians of the emperor, emphasized loyalty and the importance of a solid culture. These lessons, interwoven with modern principles of Navy SEALs and Spetsnaz, became an endless source of wisdom for forming exceptional teams. Each carefully crafted chapter became an anchor point for building high-performance teams.

From contextualizing the importance in contemporary management to the challenges faced in team formation, and from the discipline of the Mirmidons to the Roman vanguard of the Pretorians, the journey was filled with discoveries and practical applications.

As we advanced to contextualization, we explored the vital importance of high-performance teams in today's management era. We discussed challenges in assembling exceptional teams and the crucial responsibility of managers in this process. Each topic, each word, contributed to an enhanced understanding of how organizations can transcend.

Thus, our journey took us beyond conventional boundaries of management, into the hallways of the extraordinary. "Mission Given, Mission Accomplished" is not just a title; it's a mantra, a call for leaders and managers to blaze trails that transcend expectations, much like special forces do routinely.

We conclude this journey, but it is only the beginning. The timeless lessons from special forces will remain invaluable guides in building high-performance teams. May this book serve not only as a compendium of knowledge but as a catalyst for continuous transformation and excellence in all organizations seeking to surpass boundaries and achieve the extraordinary.

Technical Data: Navy SEALs

1. **Full Name:** United States Navy Sea, Air, and Land Teams (Navy SEALs)

2. **Foundation:** The Navy SEALs were officially founded in 1962.

3. **Military Branch:** United States Navy

4. **Main Mission:** Execute maritime, aerial, and land special operations in hostile environments.

5. **Motto:** "The Only Easy Day Was Yesterday"

6. **Training:**

- BUD/S (Basic Underwater Demolition/SEAL) Training: Underwater demolition and amphibious combat skills training.

- SEAL Qualification Training (SQT): SEAL qualification program.

- SEAL Advanced Training: Advanced training in weapons, navigation, combat medicine, and special tactics.

7. **Selection:**

- Rigorous selection process, including intensive physical tests, psychological evaluations, and interviews.

8. **Current Strength:** The exact number is classified, but it is estimated that there are around 2,500 to 3,000 Navy SEALs in service.

9. **Operational Base:** SEALs are based in Coronado, California (West Coast SEAL Team) and Virginia Beach, Virginia (East Coast SEAL Team).

10. Notable Operations:

- Active participation in the Vietnam War.

- Operation "Neptune Spear" - Capture of Osama bin Laden in 2011.

- Various counterterrorism missions and hostage rescues.

11. Typical Equipment:

- Advanced firearms, including assault rifles and pistols.

- Diving equipment.

- Close combat gear.

- Advanced communication equipment.

12. Core Values:

- Loyalty to the Team: Placing the team's well-being above personal interests.

- Determination: Persevering in the face of challenges, maintaining motivation and focus.

- Discipline: Adopting high standards of behavior and performance.

- Honorability: Acting with integrity and ethics in all situations.

13. Specific Skills:

- Amphibious combat operations.

- Silent infiltration and exfiltration.

- Close-quarters combat.

- Tactical parachuting.

- Land and maritime navigation.

14. Average Age: SEALs have an average age of 28 to 30 years.

15. Fun Facts:

- BUD/S training is known for its intensity, with a high dropout rate.

- The SEALs' insignia is a trident with an anchor, representing maritime capabilities, and a dagger, representing land and combat capabilities.

Technical Data: United States Army Rangers

1. **Full Name:** 75th Ranger Regiment, United States Army

2. **Foundation:** Officially activated on February 3, 1986.

3. **Military Branch:** United States Army.

4. **Main Mission:** Conduct airborne assault, ambushes, reconnaissance, search and rescue, and other special operations in hostile environments.

5. **Motto:** "Rangers Lead the Way."

6. **Training:**

- RASP (Ranger Assessment and Selection Program): Selection and assessment program for entry into the regiment.

- Ranger School: Leadership, combat skills, patrol, and survival training course.

7. **Selection:**

- Rigorous selection process, including physical tests, leadership assessments, and specialized training.

8. **Current Strength:** The exact number is classified, but it is estimated that there are around 3,500 Rangers in service.

9. **Operational Base:** Main units are based at Fort Benning, Georgia (1st Battalion), and Hunter Army Airfield, Georgia (2nd and 3rd Battalions).

10. Notable Operations:

- Active participation in the Gulf War, Afghanistan, and Iraq.

- Long-range reconnaissance and direct combat missions.

11. Typical Equipment:

- Standard U.S. Army firearms, including assault rifles and machine guns.

- Advanced communication equipment.

- Tactical and survival gear.

12. Core Values:

- Courage: Acting bravely in the face of danger.

- Leadership: Being effective leaders at all times.

- Honesty: Maintaining integrity and acting with honesty.

- Teamwork: Collaborating effectively to achieve common goals.

13. Specific Skills:

- Airborne assault.

- Combat patrol.

- Long-range reconnaissance.

- Search and rescue operations.

14. **Average Age:** The age range of Rangers varies, but many are between 18 and 35 years.

15. Fun Facts:

- Rangers are known for their quick-response capabilities and highly trained operations.

- During World War II, Rangers were famous for their actions on the Normandy beaches, known as "Pointe Du Hoc."

Technical Data: SAS (Special Air Service)

1. **Full Name:** Special Air Service (SAS)

2. **Foundation:** Formed in 1941 during World War II.

3. **Country of Origin:** United Kingdom.

4. Main Mission: Conduct special operations, including reconnaissance, sabotage, hostage rescue, and direct actions in hostile environments.

5. **Motto:** "Who Dares Wins."

6. **Selection and Training:**

- SFQC (Special Forces Qualification Course): Special Forces Qualification Course for recruits.

- SAS Selection: Notorious and rigorous selection process, including strenuous physical tests and psychological evaluations.

- SAS Training: Intensive training in combat techniques, survival, navigation, and special operations.

7. **Current Strength:** The exact number is classified, but there are estimated to be several hundred SAS operators.

8. **Operational Base:** The SAS has various units, including the headquarters in Hereford, England, and a reserve unit known as 22nd Special Air Service Regiment (22 SAS).

9. **Notable Operations:**

- Actions in World War II, Falklands, Bosnia, Iraq, and Afghanistan.

- Hostage rescues and counter-terrorism operations.

10. **Typical Equipment:**

- Variety of firearms, including assault rifles and pistols.

- Advanced tactical equipment.

- Specialized communication equipment.

11. **Core Values:**

- Courage: Facing danger with bravery.

- Integrity: Acting with honesty and ethics.

- Adaptability: Being flexible and effective in various situations.

- Teamwork: Collaborating to achieve objectives.

12. Specific Skills:

- Infiltration and exfiltration operations.

- Urban combat.

- Long-range patrol and reconnaissance.

- Counter-sabotage operations.

13. **Average Age:** SAS members have a wide age range, typically between 20 and 40 years.

14. Fun Facts:

- The SAS is one of the world's oldest special forces units.

- Participated in highly secret and notorious operations, many of which remain classified. Note: Due to the highly confidential nature of SAS operations, many specific details may not be publicly available.

Technical Data: Spetsnaz (Russian Special Forces)

1. **Full Name:** Spetsnaz (Abbreviation of "Vysokotochnye spetsialnye razvedyvatel'nye podrazdeleniya" - High-Precision Reconnaissance Units)

2. **Country of Origin:** Russia.

3. **Foundation:** Originating from the Soviet Union era but formally constituted in 1950.

4. **Main Mission:** Execute special operations, including reconnaissance, sabotage, counter-sabotage, hostage rescue, and direct actions in hostile environments.

5. **Motto:** "Смерть врагам" (Death to Enemies).

6. **Selection and Training:**

- Rigorous Selection: Extremely demanding selection process, assessing physical, mental, and psychological abilities.

- Intense Training: Comprehensive training program including hand-to-hand combat, survival, weapons techniques, and special tactics.

7. **Current Strength:** The exact number is classified, but there are estimated to be several thousand Spetsnaz operators.

8. **Operational Base:** Spetsnaz units are distributed throughout Russia and have bases in various strategic regions.

9. **Notable Operations:**

- Acted on various fronts, including the Afghan War.

- Participation in recent conflicts such as Chechnya and Syria.

- Highly confidential missions.

10. **Typical Equipment:**

- Variety of Russian weapons, including assault rifles, machine guns, and precision weapons.

- Advanced communication equipment.

- Specialized tactical equipment.

11. **Core Values:**

- Loyalty: Faithfulness to the country and assigned missions.

- Discipline: Adopting high standards of behavior and performance.

- Silence: Maintaining a discreet and confidential profile.

- Courage: Facing adverse situations with bravery.

12. Specific Skills:

- Sabotage and counter-sabotage operations.

- Deep reconnaissance in enemy territory.

- Urban combat.

- Extensive training in various climatic conditions.

13. **Average Age:** The age range of Spetsnaz members varies, generally between 20 and 35 years.

14. Fun Facts:

- Spetsnaz units are known for their robust and resilient approach.

- Maintain a tradition of secrecy and distance from public exposure. Note: Due to the highly confidential nature of Spetsnaz operations, many specific details may not be publicly available.

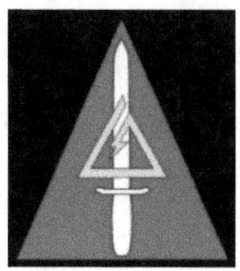

Technical Data: Delta Force
(1st Special Forces Operational
Detachment-Delta, Delta Force)

1. **Full Name:** 1st Special Forces Operational Detachment-Delta (1st SFOD-D), commonly known as Delta Force.

2. **Country of Origin:** United States.

3. **Foundation:** Officially activated in 1977, following the failed hostage rescue operation in Iran.

4. **Military Branch:** United States Army.

5. **Main Mission:** Execute counterterrorism operations, hostage rescue, reconnaissance, and other special operations in hostile environments.

6. **Motto:** (Your Obedience to Our Mission).

7. **Selection and Training:**

- Selective Selection: Highly selective selection process involving physical, psychological, and skills assessments.

- Q-Course: Participation in specialized training courses, including combat operations, parachute jumps, diving, and other specialized skills.

8. **Current Strength:** The exact number is classified, but there are estimated to be a few hundred Delta operators.

9. **Operational Base:** The exact base is classified, but the unit is believed to be located in the Fort Bragg, North Carolina area.

10. Notable Operations:

- Participation in special operations during the Gulf War, Afghanistan, and Iraq.

- Hostage rescues in various parts of the world.

- Involvement in highly confidential missions.

11. Typical Equipment:

- Advanced firearms, including assault rifles and machine guns.

- Specialized communication equipment.

- High-tech tactical equipment.

12. Core Values:

- Loyalty: Faithfulness to the mission and teammates.

- Integrity: Maintaining high ethical standards.

- Courage: Facing dangers with determination.

- Innovation: Adopting creative approaches to overcome challenges.

13. Specific Skills:

- Hostage rescue operations.

- Stealthy infiltration and exfiltration.

- Counter-sabotage operations.

- Urban combat.

14. **Average Age:** The age range of Delta Force members varies, generally between 25 and 40 years.

15. Fun Facts:

- Delta Force is one of the most secretive elite units in the U.S. military.

- The unit comprises highly trained operators from various military specialties.

  Note: Due to the highly confidential nature of Delta Force operations, many specific details may not be publicly available.

Epilogue

"From Elite to Excellence - Lessons from Special Forces for the Corporate World"

Throughout this journey into the elite of special forces, we explored the backstage of extraordinary units such as the Navy SEALs, the Rangers, the SAS, the Spetsnaz, and the Delta Force. These forces, forged in the heat of battles and extreme challenges, not only protect their nations but also offer a valuable arsenal of lessons applicable to the corporate world and contemporary management.

The Power of Rigorous Selection and Training: The strength of these units begins with the meticulous selection of their members, followed by intensive training. Just as in forming high-performance teams in organizations, careful talent identification and continuous investment in training are fundamental.

Inspiring and Motivational Leadership: The leaders of these special forces are catalysts of inspiration and motivation. From the SEALs to the SAS, effective leadership is a constant. The ability to lead, motivate, and inspire becomes a vital lesson for managers who must be beacons of inspiration in their workplaces.

Teamwork and Cohesive Culture: The success of these units depends intrinsically on teamwork and a cohesive culture. Cohesion, mutual trust, and collaboration are key elements that permeate all aspects of their operations, teaching us that organizational success is rooted in building united teams.

Resilience and Adaptation as Strategic Assets: Faced with adversities, special forces demonstrate resilience and adaptability. In the business world, where changes are constant, these lessons are invaluable. Resilience is not just about resisting but also about learning and thriving amid uncertainty.

Quick and Effective Decision-Making: In high-risk environments, decisions must be made quickly. Special forces teach us the importance of clear thinking and effective decision-making, a vital skill for managers facing dynamic challenges.

Talent Development as a Long-Term Investment: Just as special forces invest in the constant development of their members, organizations should see talent development as a lasting investment. Customized strategies, constructive feedback, and continuing education are pillars for building exceptional teams.

From Combat to Corporation - A Powerful Transition: Although the scenarios are distinct, the lessons are interchangeable. The journey of special forces from the battlefield to the office highlights that crucial skills for success have no boundaries. Discipline, ethics, innovation, and a passion for mission fulfillment transcend the most challenging environments.

Mission Accomplished: This book is a tribute to the dedication, courage, and sacrifice of special forces. May the lessons learned, the stories shared, and the outlined strategies inspire managers to lead with excellence, to form high-performance teams, and to achieve corporate missions as grand as the operations of these extraordinary forces.

Thus, we conclude this journey, remembering that the pursuit of excellence is a continuous mission, and the path to mastery never knows borders. May each manager adopt these lessons, turning challenges into opportunities and shaping teams that not only face but also overcome. The mission is given, may it be accomplished.

Management Terms Glossary

High-Performance Teams:

- **Definition:** Groups of highly qualified individuals who collaborate efficiently to achieve common goals.

- **Context:** These teams are fundamental for obtaining exceptional results in organizations.

Inspiring Leadership:

- **Definition:** Ability to influence and motivate others, providing inspiration and a clear vision.

- **Context:** An inspiring leader is vital for mobilizing and engaging teams in the pursuit of challenging goals.

Organizational Resilience:

- **Definition:** The ability of an organization to adapt and recover efficiently in the face of changes and challenges.

- **Context:** Resilience is crucial in dynamic and ever-evolving corporate environments.

Quick Decision-Making:

- **Definition:** Ability to make effective choices in a short period, often in pressure situations.

- **Context:** This skill is essential for managers facing dynamic challenges.

Talent Development:

- **Definition:** Continuous investment in identifying, enhancing, and promoting the potential of team members.

- **Context:** Talent development is crucial for building skilled and adaptable teams.

Cohesive Organizational Culture:

- **Definition:** Set of values, beliefs, and shared practices that promote cohesion and collaboration among organization members.

- **Context:** A cohesive culture is essential for building strong teams aligned with organizational objectives.

Business Innovation:

- **Definition:** Introduction of new ideas, methods, or products that contribute to the growth and enhancement of the organization.

- **Context:** Innovation is crucial to maintaining competitiveness and relevance in the market.

Constructive Feedback:

- **Definition:** Communication that provides specific assessments and guidance for personal and professional development.

- **Context:** Constructive feedback is a powerful tool for improving individual and team performance.

Intensive Training:

- **Definition:** Rigorous learning programs aimed at developing technical and behavioral skills.

- **Context:** Intensive training is crucial for building highly skilled and adaptable professionals.

Continuous Learning Culture:

- **Definition:** Organizational environment that promotes the constant pursuit of knowledge and professional improvement.

- **Context:** A culture of continuous learning is essential for innovation and adaptation in dynamic environments.

These management terms are essential for understanding the lessons and strategies discussed throughout this book, providing a solid foundation for implementing the learned practices.

Corporate Terms Glossary

Stakeholder:

- **Definition:** Any individual or group with an interest in or affected by the activities and decisions of an organization.

- **Context:** Managing relationships with stakeholders is crucial for the success and sustainability of a company.

Feedback:

- **Definition:** Information about the performance of an individual, team, or process, provided with the goal of improvement.

- **Context:** Constructive feedback is essential for professional development and continuous improvement.

Insights:

- **Definition:** Deep perceptions or understandings derived from the analysis and interpretation of data or information.

- **Context:** Insights are fundamental for informed decision-making and effective strategies.

Innovation:

- **Definition:** Introduction of something new or improved, whether in products, services, or processes.

- **Context:** Innovation is essential for the competitiveness and sustainable growth of organizations.

Operational Efficiency:

- **Definition:** Achievement of tasks and processes in an optimized manner, maximizing production with available resources.

- **Context:** Operational efficiency aims to achieve superior results with fewer resource consumptions.

Business Resilience:

- **Definition:** The ability of an organization to adapt, resist, and recover in the face of adversities and changes.

- **Context:** Resilience is crucial for the sustainability and continuity of business in challenging scenarios.

Organizational Culture:

- **Definition:** Set of values, beliefs, and behaviors shared within an organization.

- **Context:** Organizational culture influences decision-making, interactions, and the work environment.

Change Management:

- **Definition:** The process of planning and implementing significant changes in the operations or structure of an organization.

- **Context:** Effective change management is essential to minimize resistance and ensure smooth transitions.

Diversity and Inclusion:

- **Definition:** Promotion of a variety of origins, characteristics, and perspectives, aiming to create richer and more innovative environments.

- **Context:** Diversity and inclusion are crucial to drive creativity and organizational performance.

Business Agility:

- **Definition:** The ability of an organization to adapt quickly to market changes and respond promptly.

- **Context:** Agility is vital in dynamic and ever-evolving business environments.

Appendix

Tools for Reflection and Leadership Development

Discussion Guide for Study Groups

Team Development:

- How can we apply high-performance team formation strategies in our workplace?

- What are common challenges in building teams, and how can we overcome them?

Inspiring Leadership:

- What are the characteristics of an inspiring leader? Can we identify these characteristics in known leaders?

- How can we inspire and motivate our team on a daily basis?

Resilience and Adaptation:

- How does our organization deal with changes and adversities? Are there areas where we can improve?

- What strategies can we adopt to promote a culture of resilience in our team?

Quick Decision-Making:

- What is the decision-making process in our organization? Is it agile and efficient?

- How can we enhance the ability to make quick and effective decisions?

Talent Development:

- How do we identify leadership potential in our team?

- What talent development programs can be implemented in our organization?

Organizational Culture:

- What is the predominant culture in our organization? Is it aligned with our values?

- What initiatives can strengthen a cohesive and collaborative culture in our team?

Personal Reflection and Leadership Development Questions

Self-awareness:

- What are my main strengths as a leader? And what areas need development?

- How does my leadership impact the team's culture?

Personal Goals and Vision:

- What are my long-term goals as a leader? How can I work to achieve them?

- How does my personal vision align with the organization's objectives?

Communication and Feedback:

- How can I improve my communication skills with the team?

- Am I open to constructive feedback? How can I encourage a feedback culture in the team?

Decision-Making:

- How do I deal with pressure situations when making decisions?

- What are my strengths in decision-making, and where can I improve?

Team Development:

- How do I promote the individual development of each team member?

- What measures can I take to strengthen team spirit?

Resilience and Adaptation:

- How do I react to changes and challenges? What can I do to improve my resilience?

- Am I open to adapting my leadership approach as needed?

Use these reflection tools as valuable guides in your continuous development as a leader. Remember that personal reflection and open dialogue are fundamental for individual and collective growth.

Navy Seals Motivation

"What starts here changes the world."

1. Start each day with a task completed.

2. Find someone to help you through life.

3. Respect everyone.

4. Know that life is not fair.

5. You WILL fail often.

6. Take some risks.

7. Step up when times are toughest.

8. Face down the bullies.

9. Lift up the downtrodden

10. Never, ever give up.